ZERO PPM

The Quickest Way to Become
*The **No.1 in Hydraulic Fittings Market***

ZERO PPM

The Quickest Way to Become
*The **No.1 in Hydraulic Fittings Market***

NIKHIL DHAND

Available on amazonkindle

Worldwide Published by

Pendown Press
PREMIUM BUSINESS PUBLISHER

PENDOWN PRESS LLP
An ISO 9001 & ISO 14001 Certified Co.,
Regd. Office: 3767A, Kanhaiya Nagar,
Tri Nagar, Delhi-110035
Ph.: 8130886000, 9650072927
E-mail: info@pendownpress.com
Branch Office: 1A/2A, 20, Hari Sadan, Ansari Road,
Daryaganj, New Delhi-110002
Ph.: 011-45794768
Website: PendownPress.com

Edition: 2025
Price: ₹ 399
ISBN: 978-93-6338-678-5

Layout and Cover Designed by Pendown Graphics Team
Printed and Bound in India by Thomson Press India Ltd.

DEDICATION

This book is lovingly dedicated to:

Late Sh. Manohar Lal Dhand

Founder of Dhand Steels

Whose vision and courage laid the foundation of everything we build upon today.

Mr. Jai Parkash Dhand

Whose guidance, education, and unwavering support turned that foundation into a legacy.

Your values inspire every chapter of this journey toward ZERO PPM and beyond.

TABLE OF CONTENTS

PREFACE

The How, Why & What of This Book?

Why Was This Book Written?

Imagine running a hydraulic fittings business where every customer calls you first, trusts your quality blindly, and gives you repeat orders without negotiation.

At Dhand Steels, we've walked factory floors for over five decades.

We've seen rejections that broke trust, missed POs that drained morale, and teams who gave their best but still lost clients, just because of unsuitable raw material or missing systems.

This book distills everything we've learned about achieving ZERO PPM, — into practical, proven steps that any serious manufacturer can act on.

What Does ZERO PPM Really Mean?

ZERO PPM = Zero parts per million rejected.

In simple words:

- Make 10 lakh fittings, and not even 1 is defective.
- Zero customer complaints
- Zero urgent rework
- Zero brand damage

It means:

- Peace of mind for you
- Respect from your team
- Loyalty from your customer

And yes, it is **absolutely possible.**

What Can This Book Do For You?

This book is not about theory. It's built on the real problems and real solutions of Indian manufacturers just like you.

With this book, you will learn how to:

- Reduce your rejection rate to zero
- Deliver on time, every time
- Win big orders without competing on price
- Build a premium brand that customers can't ignore

By the end of this book, you'll either have a blueprint to implement all this or the confidence to partner with experts who can help you do so.

Who Is This Book For?

This book is for the unsung warriors of manufacturing — The hydraulic fittings makers who fight daily fires of rejections, urgent dispatches, quality complaints, and cash flow stress.

It's for:

- Factory owners who dream of scaling — but are stuck in operations
- Quality heads who are tired of defending defects

- Purchase and production managers looking to build trust with OEMs
- Entrepreneurs who want to make their brand stand for reliability, not excuses

Who Am I and Why Should You Trust Me?

Hi, I'm a 37-year-old engineer from Bangalore who has helped dozens of hydraulic fittings manufacturers transform from struggling with rejections to becoming zero-defect suppliers to global brands.

Through Dhand Steels, we support companies with high-quality precision steel bars and actionable process consulting.

This book isn't for copy-paste readers.

It's for **leaders** who want their shop floor to reflect the premium quality their customers expect.

If you're reading this, thank you.

Because it means you're committed to building something remarkable, not just operational.

Let's raise the bar for our teams, our customers, and India's reputation in manufacturing.

— Nikhil Dhand
For Team Dhand Steels.

A DISCLAIMER

This book shares strategic insights, real-world stories, and industry wisdom gathered from years of experience helping hydraulic fittings manufacturers achieve near-zero rejections and scalable growth.

The intent is to inspire, educate, and guide — not to publicly disclose proprietary processes, vendor details, or confidential methodologies.

While examples and frameworks are shared to illustrate principles, the full implementation systems, detailed SOPs, quality checklists, vendor networks, and in-house innovations are only available to verified partners and clients of Dhand Steels.

Readers are encouraged to reach out if they are serious about implementing the Zero Defect approach and transforming their manufacturing ecosystem.

Knowledge Protects. Execution Transforms..

CHAPTER 1

MYTHS THAT KEEP YOU STUCK

Every factory starts with big dreams — growth, quality, repeat clients.

But over time, subtle beliefs sneak in. Beliefs that feel normal, safe, and logical.

The Truth?

These same beliefs quietly block your growth and damage your brand — until one day, your top client stops calling, and you don't even know why.

Picture This...

You're negotiating with a local supplier.
The rate is fantastic. The steel looks shiny.
You think to yourself,
"Loha toh loha hi hota hai." (All material is the same.)
You place the order.
Four weeks later –
You're firefighting rejections, chasing your QC team, and wondering what went wrong.

The Myths That Sound Right (But Hurt You Badly)

- "*Loha toh loha hi hota hai.* (All material is the same at the end of the day!)"
- "2-4 *pcs reject ho jaaye toh koi baat nahi.* (A few pieces being rejected is no big deal)"
- "*Quality team sab dekh legi.* (The quality team will take care of everything)"
- "*Raw Material ka Rate kam mila toh profit zyada hoga.* (Paying less for raw material will give more profits)"

What These Beliefs Actually Do

- Rejections silently increase, leading to client frustration.
- QC shifts from being a controller to a firefighter.
- Operators lose faith in leadership due to recurring issues.
- Clients start expecting problems in every order, damaging trust.

The Reality (No Filter)

- Quality begins at the raw material gate, not at the dispatch table.
- A rejected batch costs more than the entire margin you saved.
- Trust, once lost, cannot be regained with discounts.
- Steel chemistry, gas levels, and tolerances are more critical than surface shine.

How to Escape the Myth Trap:

- Start demanding UT, MTC, and Gas Composition reports
- Audit your steel supplier like you audit your top client

- Educate your purchase and QC team on the cost of poor quality (COPQ)
- Log every rejection and trace it back to the actual cause, not the person

A Real-World Biz Story

₹ 25 L Lost (Then Recovered) by Upgrading One Belief

"I was saving ₹10 per kg. But losing lakhs in silence."
— Prakash Tiwari

Prakash prided himself on getting "the best rates." But within 4 months, two major clients paused orders worth ₹ 25 L. Turns out, the steel he ordered, though shiny and smooth, had uncontrolled gas content, re-rolled grain structure, and inconsistent carbon.

After switching to Dhand Steels' certified bright bars with traceable reports, and implementing rejection tagging at dispatch:

- Switched to Dhand Steels' certified bright bars with traceable reports
- Implemented rejection tagging at dispatch
- **The rejection rate dropped from 14% to 1.6%**
- **OEM client returned with double the order**
- The QC team began flagging issues before they reached production

A Challenge for You

- **Ask your QC team:** What were the top 3 reasons for rejection last month?
  - **Ask your vendor:** Can you show me one batch's UT + Gas Report?
  - **Ask yourself:** Am I leading by margin — or by mindset?

A Key Lesson

You don't need new machines. You need to upgrade your beliefs before you upgrade your tools.

CHAPTER 2

INCONSISTENT DIMENSIONS
(WHY 0.2 MM CAN COST YOU CRORES)

You've invested in machines. Your operators are trained.

You trust your team.

Still, your best client complains: "***Leak ho raha hai***. (The product is leaking)"

You're confused — and hurt.

Everything checked out... **so where did it go wrong?**

It's time to look deeper — not just at what you see, but at what you don't check often enough.

Picture This...

You just shipped a **₹6 lakh** batch.

Two days later, your client calls — angry.

"Sir, seal proper nahi baith raha."

(Sir, the seal doesn't fit properly.)

Your QC report says all dimensions are within range.

But in the world of hydraulics,

±0.1 mm is all it takes to ruin a connection.

What Most Teams Say

- *"Final inspection mein sab theek tha.* (Everything was okay in the last inspection)."
- *"CNC pe kaam ho raha hai, accurate hi hoga.* (The work must be good as it is being done on CNC)"
- *"Itna chhota difference client ko kya pata chalega?* (The client won't be able to spot such a minute difference.)"
- *"Machine operator experienced hai, woh dekh lega.* (The machine operator is experienced; he will manage everything.) "

But What's Really Happening?

- Dimensional checks are performed at the end of the process, rather than mid-process.
- Operators are not logging or tagging variations accurately.
- Raw bars often have tolerance issues right from the start.
- Tool wear gradually causes dimensions to drift out of specification.

How to Fix the Invisible Drift

- Use GO/NO-GO gauges every 30 pieces
- Set up a 3-point inspection SOP (start, mid, end)
- Track actual vs spec in a visible log (whiteboard/Excel)
- Only use bright bars with h11 tolerance (not "approx")
- Conduct tool wear audits every 3 days

A Real-World Biz Story

Client Returned. Team Got Promoted.

"We realized – *machine se zyada, measurement system ka upgrade zaroori tha.*"

– Mr. Akash·Mehra, Production Head

Akash had a decent setup — CNCs, QC, digital gauges. Still, rejection was at 18%. Clients blamed him. The problem? Raw bars were varying. Checks were delayed. They were "blindly trusting" the machines.

We supplied Dhand Steels bright bars (with **verified h11 tolerance**), trained the team to check mid-batch, and built a visual log system.

Within 3 months:

- Rejection dropped to 1.2% within 3 months
- OEM reinstated ₹30L order
- The QC team leader got promoted to Production Lead

A Challenge For You

- Walk to your floor and ask to see the last batch dimension log.
- Consult your tool room to find out when the last three tool replacements were done.
- Verify with your QC team whether they have the authority to pause production.

A Key Lesson

Your machine may not lie — but if no one's checking the truth, your client won't believe you either.

CHAPTER 3

SUBSTANDARD RAW MATERIAL (THE ROOT YOU NEVER QUESTION)

You're doing everything right.

Machines are calibrated. SOPs are in place. Operators are skilled.

Still, you face random issues — cracked threads, early rusting, and tool breakage.

You suspect machining, plating, QC...

But the Real Culprit?

The raw material you trusted, without truly checking.

Picture This...

A batch goes for plating. Looks perfect.

A week later, it comes back with tiny cracks.

You double-check drawings, threading, and tool life.

Everything seems fine — until you test the steel itself.

And boom

It's filled with internal stress, high sulphur, and inconsistent hardness.

Why Most Factories Never Catch This

- "*Vendor wahi hai, saalon se*. (The vendor has been with us for years)"
- "*Steel chamak raha hai — toh acha hi hoga*. (The steel must be good since it is shining so much.)"
- "Lab test mein paisa kyun waste karein? (Why waste money on a lab test?)"
- "Client ne kabhi poocha nahi. (The client never asks.)"

But This Is What It's Costing You

- Threads peel or crack under torque
- Pressure test fails after dispatch
- Machines break tools too soon
- Plating doesn't stick properly
- Your brand loses trust, silently

How to Never Be Trapped Again

- Ask for full MTC (NABL Test Certificate) — every batch
- Demand a UT (Ultrasonic Test) Report to catch hidden cracks
- Track gas content: $O_2 < 20$ ppm, $H_2 < 2$ ppm, $N_2 < 30$ ppm
- Control Sulphur/phosphorus (S & P < 0.025%)
- Reject any material without documented traceability
- Use steel made from virgin billets — no re-rolled scrap

CHAPTER 4

SURFACE FINISH PROBLEMS (THE FIRST IMPRESSION THAT CAN COST YOU EVERYTHING)

You've done the machining. Threads are accurate.

Dimensions are spot on.

But when your client opens the box, their reaction is:

"Yeh fitting ka finish kya hai? Lagta hai kisi local vendor se banwaya hai..."

(What kind of finish is this? Looks like it comes from a substandard local vendor.)

The job is functional — but the **first impression fails.**

And in today's world, **bad finish = bad brand.**

Picture This...

A ₹3L order lands on your OEM client's floor.

You expect a repeat PO. Instead, they reject 30%:

The surface has drag lines

Plating is inconsistent

Threads feel rough

The Cause?

- Surface Ra was above 2.0 µm.
- Too high for their hydraulic seal expectations.

You just lost a valuable client over the first impression.

What Most Shops Say

- "*Surface finish se kya hota hai? Kaam toh karta hai.* (How does surface finish matter so long as it is working?)"
- "*Tool change abhi toh hua tha.* (We just changed the tool.)"
- "*Mirror polish sirf show-off hai.* (Mirror polish is mere showoff.)"
- "*Finish mein paisa waste kyon karein?* (Why waste money on the finish?)"

These excuses are why exports fail silently.

The Real Problem Lies Beneath the Surface

- High Ra = O-ring leakage, bad coating, client distrust
- Drag lines = poor lubrication + dull tools
- Rough threads = failed seal test
- Finish = visual trust + technical tolerance

Acid Pickling Creates Surface Pits

Yes, acid pickling cleans scales, **but:**

- It etches the steel unevenly
- Leads to microscopic pits on the bar
- These pits trap plating chemicals, moisture, and dust

- **The result?**
  - Poor coating adhesion
  - Higher Ra
  - Early rusting

Acid pickling may look clean, but it weakens your foundation, especially for precision parts.

The Better Alternative: Shot Blasting (Done Right)

Modern shot blasting:

- Uses abrasive impact to clean the surface
- Avoids chemical handling
- Produces a matte, uniform, pit-free finish
- Ra remains stable when paired with:
  - Fresh tooling
  - Clean coolant
  - Proper thread polishing

How to Master Finish Without Acid

- Use shot-blasted bright bars from a trusted vendor
- Check Ra using a profilometer
- Replace tools before they scar the surface
- Use clean, filtered coolant
- Mirror polish thread zones for OEM parts
- Final clean with air blast — never hand rub
- VCI wrap + dry box for corrosion-free delivery

A Real-World Biz Story

From Rough to Remarkable with Shot-Blasted Steel

"We didn't just change bars.

We changed how the client saw us."

– Rajeev Malhotra, Head of Quality

Rajeev's fittings worked mechanically, but failed visually. A German OEM rejected an entire shipment.

Reason?

"Surface is dull. Threads feel rough. No premium feel."

Audit showed:

- Acid-pickled bars → surface pits
- High Ra values (>2.0 µm)
- Threads weren't polished
- Final cleaning was manual

We recommended:

Switch to shot-blasted bars with Ra < 1.2 µm

Profilometer-based QC

Mirror polish for critical sealing zones

No-contact packaging SOP

Results Within 45 Days:

- Visual rejections dropped by 94%
- Client reinstated orders
- 3 new buyers impressed by product photos
- Rajeev promoted to Plant Head

A Challenge For You

- **Ask your vendor:** Are you getting acid-pickled or shot-blasted bars?
- **Measure Ra before and after polishing** — do you see a drop?
- **Ask your QC:** How many visual rejections were logged last month?

A Key Lesson

Surface finish isn't cosmetic — it's conversion power.

And sometimes, it's the difference between

"Send next PO" and "Let's pause this vendor."

CHAPTER 5

THREADING FAILURES (THE HIDDEN KILLER OF FITTINGS)

You've checked the dimensions. You've ensured the surface finish. You even got the best raw material.

But clients still complain: ***"Threads crack ho gaye."*** *"Seal nahi ho raha properly." "Hydraulic test fail ho gaya."*

(**"Threads have cracked**. It doesn't seal properly. It has failed the hydraulic test.")

The threads — your most critical interface — are often the most neglected.

Picture This...

Your client assembles a fitting. They tighten it, expecting a perfect seal.

Instead, they hear a crack — or worse, a slow leak under 300 bar pressure.

Dangerous Myths About Threading Accuracy

- "*Threading toh machine se ho raha hai, galti kaise hogi?* (The threading is done by machine, then how can it go wrong?)"
- "We checked with thread ring — toh perfect hai (it was perfect)."
- "*Thread depth thoda adjust kar lo, chalega.* (Just adjust the thread depth a bit, it'll work.)"
- "Client ne tighten galat kiya hoga. (The client must have tightened it wrongly.)"

The Silent Killers of Thread Quality

- Threads chip when hardness is above 28 HRC
- Thread finish too rough = leakage or galling
- No GO/NO-GO = no real QC
- Threads are blamed last, but cause most failures

Best Practices That Save You from Thread Rejections

- Use GO/NO-GO plug or ring gauges every 50 pieces
- Use high-speed steel (HSS) or carbide threading inserts
- Maintain bar hardness below **180 BHN** (≈ **20 HRC**) for proper thread formation. High hardness (> 26 HRC) can cause tool breakage and cracked threads
- Always apply cutting oil/lube during threading
- Replace the thread tool before visible wear
- Check the thread pitch diameter with a micrometer or profile projector
- Run a pressure test on random samples every day

A Challenge For You

- **Go to your shop floor:** When was the last thread tool changed?
- **Ask your QC:** How often are GO/NO-GO gauges used?
- **Pick 5 fittings:** do a profile projector check today

A Key Lesson

The thread is your handshake with the client. Make sure it's strong, clean, and precise — or your deal might slip through the cracks..

CHAPTER 6

COATING & RUST ISSUES (THE SILENT KILLER OF TRUST)

You've shipped the parts. They were clean.

They passed pressure tests. Everyone is happy.

Until... a week later, your client calls: ***"Sir, aapke fittings mein rust aa gaya."*** (Sir, your fittings are rusted.)

> **Picture This...**
>
> 800 fittings packed in VCI bags, shipped to Germany.
>
> **5 rusted.**
>
> **The entire ₹ 10 L shipment was rejected.**

Common Excuses That Blind You to Rust Risks

- "*Packing sahi tha, toh rust kahan se aaya*? (The packing was perfect, then where did the rust come from?)"
- "*Client ka warehouse hi damp hoga.*" (The client's warehouse must be damp.)
- "1–2 *piece rust ho gaya toh kya farak padta hai*? (A few pieces getting rusted is not such a big deal.)"

These excuses may save your ego today –

But they **cost you trust and orders tomorrow.**

Why Rust Happens (Even When You Think It Shouldn't)

- Plating adhesion is weak due to high Ra or poor surface prep
- Micro-cracks in raw bars = moisture trap
- Improper drying before packing = rust formation
- No salt spray = no validation
- Silent rust = slow brand death

How to Rust-Proof Your Reputation

- Use polished bright bars (Ra < 1.2 μm)
- Work only with ASTM B633 / ISO 4042-certified coating vendors
- Salt spray test – minimum 72 hours, weekly
- Warm air drying after plating, before packing
- Final packing: VCI paper + desiccant + dry box
- 24-hour damp cloth test on random samples

A Real-World Biz Story

Rust Rejection Became a ₹90L Comeback

"We lost one shipment, but gained a system. Now, rust isn't even in our vocabulary."
– Ramesh Hydraulics, Jabalpur

Issue: Export consignment to Germany rejected on arrival due to rust.

Investigation showed

- Substandard plating
- Bar micro-cracks
- Zero salt spray validation

It wasn't just about one shipment — it was a systemic failure.

They acted fast

- Switched to low-Ra, UT-tested bars
- Upgraded to global-compliant coating vendors
- Introduced full drying + VCI packing SOPs
- Made salt spray testing non-negotiable

The Outcome

- Became the preferred vendor for the same German client
- Received a ₹90L repeat order
- Zero rust complaints since
- SOP was adopted across their group companies

A Challenge For You

- When did you last run a salt spray test?
- Do you inspect coating thickness regularly?
- Are your bars UT-tested before plating?

A Key Lesson

Rust isn't just about red spots.

It's about the red flags your client raises when it's already too late.

CHAPTER 7

FINAL QUALITY CHECKS (WHY DEFECTS ESCAPE AND WHAT TO DO ABOUT IT)

You've done everything right — or so you thought.

Yet a cracked fitting still makes it to the client.

QC had stamped it **'OK'**. But was it really?

This chapter isn't about **doing** a final inspection.

It's about doing it **right — every single time.**

> **Picture This...**
>
> You proudly dispatch a ₹12 L order.
>
> **A few days later, a complaint.**

The Client Finds

➢ A cracked fitting

➢ The thread doesn't match

➢ QC stamp says "Passed"

You're shocked.

The Reality?

➢ Poor lighting in the inspection area

➢ No MPI (Magnetic Particle Inspection)

- An **untrained helper** applied the 'OK' stamp

Now, the price of "**casual QC**"?

A ruined relationship.

Excuses That Sabotage the Final QC

- "*Final QC mein sab theek tha*. (Everything was okay in the final QC.)"
- "*Last minute mein jaldi karna pada*. (Last-minute hurry caused this.)"
- "*Crack toh plating ke baad dikha hoga*. (The crack must have shown up after plating.)"
- "*Helper ne hi toh stamp kiya — minor issue hoga*. (The helper has stamped it, must be a minor issue.)"

These aren't explanations — they're silent killers of your brand.

Root Causes Behind Failed Final QC:

- No standard for **100% visual and dimensional checks**
- The QC table has **poor lighting**
- Thread pitch is often **not tested**
- The stamp was applied without inspection
- No initials or traceability in the QC log
- No system to **flag or hold** doubtful parts

How to Make 'Passed' Truly Mean Passed:

- Install **white LED inspection lights** at the QC station
- Use **MPI** or dye penetrant for internal cracks
- Perform **GO/NO-GO thread checks** for every lot

- Introduce a **red table system** for doubtful parts
- Give the QC team the **dispatch stop authority**
- Maintain QC logs with **operator initials and date**
- Conduct **weekly QC audits** of random samples

A Real-World Biz Story

From Red Flags to The Red Carpet

"Now, when we say 'Passed',
It actually means Passed with confidence."
– JPHydro Components, Raipur

Problem: German buyer raised consistent QC complaints – surface defects, cracked fittings, and wrong threads.

Audit revealed

- No proper lighting at the QC desk
- No MPI testing
- 'OK' stamp is often applied by a helper without checks

Actions Taken

- Installed full LED QC setup
- Brought in the MPI vendor weekly
- Set up a red table with a tag system
- Empowered the QC team to reject dispatches
- Trained operators to **log initials per check**

The Outcome

- Zero QC-related complaints in 90 days
- Client upgraded them to **Tier-1 global supplier**
- QC Head promoted as **Group Quality Coordinator**

A Challenge For You

- When did you last audit lighting at your QC stations?
- Can your QC team stop a dispatch?
- Are your inspection logs traceable and signed?

A Key Lesson

Final inspection isn't a formality — It's the last guard between your brand and the buyer's anger.

It's your last defense — and your client's first point of judgment.

CHAPTER 8

BOOSTING PRODUCTIVITY (MORE OUTPUT WITHOUT MORE MACHINES)

Orders are rising. You think you need more machines or manpower. But most factories aren't using even 70% of their real capacity.

Picture This...

Your order book is packed.
Every machine is running.
Your team is tired, **yet dispatches are delayed.**

You Dig Deeper and Find

- Setup time? 25 minutes per shift
- Tools break mid-batch
- No backup operator when someone is absent
- Jobs are sequenced randomly

You think the solution is "Let's buy a new machine."

But the truth is — you're only using 60% of what you already have.

The Lies That Keep You Stuck

- *"Naya machine le lete hain, output badh jaayega (Let's buy a new machine. The output will increase)."*
- *"Operator expert hai, system ki zaroorat nahi (The operator is an expert, no further systems are needed)."*
- *"Har banda apna kaam jaanta hai — wohi kaafi hai (Every person is skilled in their work, and that is enough)."*

These are not decisions — they are delays wearing a disguise.

What's Actually Going Wrong

- Setup time is untracked and too long
- No cross-training = panic when someone's absent
- No visibility into real-time output or targets
- Job sequencing is reactive, not planned
- Downtime is invisible — and expensive

Fix It With Flow, Not Force

- Create SOPs for setup, changeover, and startup
- Cross-train your second line — avoid single-person dependency
- Plan jobs weekly, not daily
- Use high-quality bars that extend tool life
- Track and log every minute of downtime
- Install a visual dashboard — even a whiteboard with targets vs. achieved

A Real-World Biz Story

Doubled Output Without a Single New Machine

"Productivity didn't come from pressure. It came from visibility."

- Ramesh Hydraulics, Bhopal

Situation: Output stuck at 180 pcs/day despite 4 machines and 8 operators.

They considered buying another machine - but instead called us.

Diagnosis

- Setup time untracked
- No shift-wise targets
- Operators didn't know daily goals
- Downtime wasn't even recorded

Fixes

- SOPs are laminated at each station
- Shift-based whiteboard dashboards
- Introduced the cross-training matrix
- Switched to Dhand Steels' high-precision bars

The Outcome

- Output jumped to 365 pcs/day
- On-time delivery rate up by 40%
- Investment diverted to team training, not machinery
- Ramesh decided: "No more machines till we hit 95% efficiency."

A Challenge For You

- Do you log actual vs. target output daily?
- Is there a clear SOP for changeovers and breakdowns?
- Does every operator know what success looks like?

A Key Lesson

Your factory doesn't need more machines.

It needs more clarity, consistency, and confidence.

CHAPTER 9

THE PROFIT FORMULA
(WHERE QUALITY, SPEED & PLANNING MEET)

More production ≠ , more profit.

Real profit comes from the right output, right cost, and right timing. This chapter breaks down the **formula:**

Throughput – Inventory – Expense.

> **Picture This...**
>
> You proudly complete a ₹10 L order.
> **You expect ₹ 2 L profit.**
>
> But after all the expenses... **only ₹60K is left.**

Where did it go?

- ₹ 1.5 L stuck in overstocked raw material
- ₹50 K lost in rework
- ₹70 K burned on untracked tool replacement

You **didn't lose money**.

You **lost visibility**.

Profit-Killing Myths That Sound Right

- "More orders = more profit."
- "Profit = selling price – raw material."
- "Inventory is an asset, not an expense."
- "Rework is normal."
- "Tool change toh chalta hai."

These beliefs may feel logical —

But they quietly eat your margins.

What's Actually Draining Your Profit

- Excess inventory blocks working capital
- Rework & scrap silently kill efficiency
- Tool cost rises without tracking usage
- Delays result in penalties, lost clients
- You're busy, but not always profitable

The Real Profit Formula

Profit = Throughput – Inventory Cost – Operational Expense

- Maximize defect-free throughput
- Fewer reworks = higher earnings per hour

Apply the formula:

Inventory = DAC (Daily Avg. Consumption) × Lead Time × Safety Factor

- Reduce scrap and rework with real-time analysis
- Track cost per part weekly, not just monthly
- Create a visual dashboard: Scrap %, Rework Cost, Tool Spend

A Real-World Biz Story

₹7L Recovered Without Selling a Single Extra Fitting

"We didn't grow profit by working harder
- We grew it by seeing clearer."
- SamFlex India, Nagpur

Sandeep noticed profit margins shrinking despite rising orders.

We conducted a cost mapping session.

Revealed

- Overstocked fittings: ₹ 3.2 L
- Rework cost in hidden repairs: ₹ 1.2 L
- Scrap is not being monitored
- The tool budget exceeded silently for over 3 months

Fixes

- Used DAC-based inventory logic
- Tagged scrap with cause + cost
- Tracked tool usage per operator
- Launched a live Profit Tracker Board

Results in 45 Days

- ₹ 7 L recovered from internal leaks
- Scrap fell below 1%
- Cash flow unlocked
- Managers started treating profit as a process

A Challenge For You

- What's your current cost per part, and is it accurate?
- Do you audit your scrap bins with root cause?
- Have you applied the inventory formula to even 1 item?

A Key Lesson

Profit doesn't lie in your order book.

It lies in your shopfloor systems — and how often you question them.

CHAPTER 10

INVENTORY PLANNING (UNLOCK CASH WITHOUT SELLING MORE)

Most factories don't suffer from a lack of orders — they suffer from cash stuck on shelves.

Inventory feels like safety. But without a strategy, it quietly becomes your **biggest liability.**

This chapter shows how to turn your stockroom into a profit powerhouse.

> ## Picture This...
>
> Your production is smooth. But your finance team says:
> > **"No cash for raw material this month."**

You check your store.

And there it is:

- ₹ 18 L in slow-moving stock
- Duplicate orders
- Expired packing material
- Rusted M12 blanks that nobody claimed

You don't need a loan.

You need an inventory **rethink**.

Inventory Beliefs That Trap Your Capital

- "*Stock zyada hai toh tension nahi.* (Excess stock is not a problem.)"
- "*Client demand kabhi bhi aa sakta hai.* (Client demand can come at any time.)"
- "*Bulk mein lena sasta padta hai.* (Buying in bulk is cheaper.)"
- "*Vendor ne rate kam diya tha – extra le liya.* (The vendor gave us a great rate, so we bought extra material.)"

What Happens When You Don't Plan Inventory

- Overstock = blocked cash and wasted space
- Items expire or rust quietly
- Reordering errors become frequent
- Confusion during dispatch
- Missed opportunities due to tight cash flow

How to Make Inventory Work for You

- Calculate DAC (Daily Average Consumption) for the top 30 items
- Apply formula: Inventory = DAC × Lead Time × Safety Factor
- Create Min/Max levels for each critical item
- Buy bulk at a good rate, but ask your vendor for staggered delivery
- Visual stock board: Red = reorder urgent, Yellow = reorder, Green = safe, Purple = overstock
- Train the store team to verify before every purchase

A Real-World Biz Story

₹18L Released Without Selling a Thing

**"Our store didn't need more space.
It needed more sense."
- SURYA Tech Hydraulics, Indore**

The Issue

- Frequent urgent payment requests
- M12 bars stocked for 4 months
- Same item ordered twice
- Packing boxes expired in storage

The Fix

- Applied the DAC-based inventory formula
- Switched to vendor-delivered small lots every 10 days
- Set up a Red-Yellow-Green-Purple board in stores
- Introduced a purchase approval SOP

They still bought in bulk, but asked the vendor to deliver in parts.

The Outcome:

- ₹ 18 L of stock reused, liquidated, or delayed
- 40% drop in order size — no missed dispatches
- SOP has now been rolled out in 2 more units

A Challenge For You

- List your top 10 highest-value stock items
- Calculate the ideal inventory using the DAC formula
- Check: what's lying untouched for 30+ days?

A Key Lesson

Buy smart. Store smarter.

Bulk buying isn't the problem — random stocking is.

CHAPTER 11

CONTROLLING EXPENSES (EVERY RUPEE YOU SAVE IS A RUPEE YOU EARN)

You focus on generating sales. But do you know what's silently killing your margins?

Your losses aren't always big mistakes — they're unseen leaks, draining you drop by drop.

This chapter reveals how to track, plug, and profit from those hidden drains.

> **Picture This...**
>
> You bill ₹ 25 L this month. You expect ₹ 4 L profit.
>
> You get... just ₹ 1.5 L. Where did the rest go?

You trace it and discover:

- Tools were replaced 40% earlier than needed
- Energy wastage via air leaks
- Scrap bins filled with untagged rejections
- Vendor quietly increased prices over 3 months

You didn't overspend. You just didn't notice the leaks.

Common Expense Myths That Cost You Lakhs

- "*Tool life fix nahi hoti – depends on use*. (Tool life is not fixed; it depends on usage.)"
- "*Electricity toh fixed overhead hai – kya karenge*? (Electricity is a fixed overhead; we can do nothing about it.)"
- "*Thoda scrap toh hota hi hai*. (Some amount of scrap is okay.)"
- "*Vendor pe bharosa hai – rates check karne ki zarurat nahi*. (We trust the vendor and don't need to cross-check the rates.)"

What's Draining Your Bottom Line

- Tool misuse = high cost per part
- Scrap = pure loss with zero feedback
- Power bills inflated by hidden equipment leaks
- Vendor overcharging with no alerts
- Rework never analyzed = repeated mistakes

How to Control Costs Like a Pro

- Track tool life with cost/part calculation
- Run machine-level electricity audits (clamp meter)
- Tag every scrap piece with reason, shift, and operator
- Compare vendor rates every 2–3 months
- Conduct monthly cross-department expense reviews
- Make waste visible – post weekly loss figures on the board

A Real-World Biz Story

₹8 L Saved by Fixing Leaks, Not Chasing Sales

"Our profit didn't grow by selling more.
It grew by leaking less."
– Max Solutions, Rajkot

Their sales were strong, but their profit wasn't.
We did a waste-mapping session. What showed up?

- Tools are being overused and breaking unpredictably
- Scrap not categorized — just thrown away
- Compressors running 24x7
- The vendor raised the cutting fluid price by 18% — unnoticed

What changed

- Introduced tool life tags per machine
- Weekly scrap report with reasons
- Electricity audit + compressor timer setup
- Vendor cost dashboard launched

The Outcome

- ₹ 8 L recovered in just 60 days
- Profit margin jumped from 9% → 14%
- Ramesh's practices were scaled across 3 plants

A Challenge For You

- When did you last review the tool cost per part?
- Are all rejections tagged with a root cause?
- Is your vendor price history logged?

A Key Lesson

Efficiency isn't about working harder. It's about losing less and learning more.

A SPECIAL GLIMPSE OF THE ZERO PPM CHECKLIST

Before you go, here's a quick preview of what your full checklist will look like:

Quality Checks

- Are all raw materials MTC + UT + gas tested?
- Is the Ra value consistently below 1.6 μm?
- Are GO/NO-GO gauges used in every shift?

Process Discipline

- Do you have SOPs for setup, changeover, and QC?
- Is tool change tracked per machine/operator?

Coating & Packing

- Do your coated parts pass salt spray for 72 hours?
- Is final packing done with VCI + desiccant?

Cost & Planning

- Is inventory calculated using DAC × Lead Time × SF?
- Do you track cost per part weekly?

*This is just a glimpse. The complete, ready-to-use checklist includes over 35 critical points across quality, process, planning, and profit.

Download the Full Checklist & Kickstart Your ZERO PPM Journey

➢ **Get your full, editable checklist here:**

www.dhandsteels.com/zero-ppm-checklist

YOUR TWO CHOICES

You've now read the full **ZERO PPM blueprint.** You've seen how small changes in quality, process, and material can lead to massive results — more profit, less stress, and unmatched customer loyalty.

At this point, you have two powerful options in front of you:

1. Do It Yourself

Take the insights from this book, implement the strategies on your own, and begin your journey to **ZERO PPM independently.**

If you're disciplined and ready to invest the time, you absolutely can succeed. Use the roadmap, apply the checklist, and keep improving step by step.

2. Partner with Dhand Steels

Let your ZERO PPM journey begin the smart way — by switching to high-trust, zero-defect steel.

We don't just sell material.

We partner with selected manufacturers who use our bars **and** want to grow with us.

What you get:

- Access to **zero-defect raw material** (already trusted by OEMs)
- Tailored guidance to optimize your process **around our bars**
- Training and quality gates that are **exclusive to our customers**

We don't offer generic consulting.

We **build long-term supply + success relationships.**

That's why the clients who switch to Dhand Steels stay with the system, not just the steel.

Take the Next Step

Ready to begin your ZERO PPM journey?

- **Chat with us directly:** +91 62838 38475
- **Email us at:** solutions@dhandsteels.com
- **Visit us online:** www.dhandsteels.com

To the future of **zero defects and premium profits,** we look forward to walking this journey with you.